T0312517

AMERICA'S
GREAT
REVIVALS

AMERICA'S
GREAT
REVIVALS

The Story of Spiritual Revival
in the United States, 1734–2000

BETHANYHOUSE

a division of Baker Publishing Group
Minneapolis, Minnesota

Previously published material from *Christian Life* magazine, © by Sunday Magazine, Inc.

"Twentieth-Century Revivals" © 2020 by Baker Publishing Group

Published by Bethany House Publishers
11400 Hampshire Avenue South
Bloomington, Minnesota 55438
www.bethanyhouse.com

Bethany House Publishers is a division of
Baker Publishing Group, Grand Rapids, Michigan

Printed in the United States of America

Library of Congress Cataloging-in-Publication Control Number: 2020933938

ISBN 978-0-7642-3499-6

Reprinted in part from *Christian Life* magazine

Unless otherwise indicated, Scripture quotations are from the *New King James Version* of the Bible. Copyright © 1982 by Thomas Nelson, Inc. Used by permission. All rights reserved.

Scripture quotations identified KJV are from the King James Version of the Bible.

Cover design by Eric Walljasper

20 21 22 23 24 25 26   7 6 5 4 3 2 1

Contents

one

A Great Awakening Stirs the Colonies

In the Massachusetts village of Northampton, a black-gowned Congregational pastor knelt in prayer. He was burdened for the 1,100 souls of the little town who, he was convinced, were afflicted with the deadly spiritual disease of the day. In a very few minutes he would be mounting the pulpit. Should he mouth the cushioning assurances that they wanted to hear, that God had selected them for salvation and eternal life and all was well with their souls? Or should he tell them what he really believed—that unless they had definitely experienced the new birth through faith in Jesus Christ, they were heading straight for hell?

The decision was made. The tall, thin-faced man arose, adjusted his periwig, and entered the little meetinghouse.

That day in 1734 marked the birth of what in many respects was the most notable revival of religion America has ever experienced. Nothing like it had happened before. Nothing quite like it has happened since.

The conditions that pressed Jonathan Edwards to his knees that Sunday seemed dark indeed. Gone was the God-fearing generation that had settled the land of America. The new generation had forgotten God. Immorality, debauchery, and self-interest ruled. Few cared about the next world. Even those who held to the externals of traditional religion had lost the heart of it.

Church membership rolls were shrinking. Conditions had become so bad in 1662 that leading ministers of Massachusetts Colony did something they thought would help, but actually made things worse. They adopted what was called the "Halfway Covenant." People who could show no evidence of a personal conversion experience still could get their children baptized as long as they could agree to the doctrine of faith and were not "scandalous in life." When the children grew up, if *they* couldn't testify to a personal conversion, only one privilege was denied—they could not partake of the Lord's Supper.

These halfway members soon exceeded the members in full communion. Halfway membership was socially acceptable. Why bother about going all the way? Eventually the prohibition from the Lord's Supper dropped away, and soon halfway covenanters trickled into the ministry.

There was a remnant of the godly left. They soon realized that the Halfway Covenant was a terrible mistake. Something revolutionary was needed to prevent the flickering flame of vital Christianity from being wholly snuffed out.

As He so often does, God chose a man to unlatch the windows of darkened churches to let in the light. That man was Jonathan Edwards.

The son of a minister, Edwards had a spiritual bent early in life. He spent hours in the woods observing nature. (His essay on the flying spider is still highly regarded.) He even built a tree house where he went to pray with his friends.

Edwards Asks Questions

But in his adolescence, Edwards began to ask questions. What kind of God is the God of creation? He found it hard to accept the stern doctrines of predestination and the sovereignty of God.

The struggle continued during his student years at Yale and nearly ruined his health. Agonizingly, he searched for assurance of salvation. Day after day, he sought God, but it seemed he was getting nowhere. Then, finally, he came upon this passage in the apostle Paul's letter to Timothy: "Now to the King eternal, immortal, invisible, to God who alone is wise, be honor and glory forever and ever. Amen" (1 Timothy 1:17).

Through that one sentence, Edwards was brought "to a new sense of things"—a sense of the glory and presence of God that was distinct from anything he had ever experienced. He longed to be "rapt up to Him in heaven, and be as it were swallowed up in Him forever!"

Edwards was at peace. It was the beginning of a new life of submission to God—both as a God of love and a God of justice.

Five years later he completed his theological studies and accepted the pastorate of the Congregational Church of Northampton, Massachusetts. His predecessor was Samuel Stoddard, his grandfather. It was Stoddard who first opened the way to the Communion Table for those who showed no sign of personal conversion, provided only that they were not "scandalous" in their way of life. Let "the unregenerate" come to the Lord's Table, he had argued, for it may help him. "Stoddard's Way" had soon been accepted by most New England churches.

12

Edwards grew increasingly concerned about the state of affairs in his parish. In 1734, he began a series of sermons on justification by faith alone. He swept away the hopes of heaven upon which so many in his congregation had been resting. Their morality, their membership in the church through the Halfway Covenant, their partaking of the Lord's Supper—all this availed nothing toward salvation. They were made to see that God had not appointed anything for them to do before coming to Christ by faith and that all their previous works were unacceptable in His sight.

With no letup, Edwards hammered home an awe-inspiring concept of God's sovereignty. As sinners, they deserved instant damnation, except for the mercy of God. There was nothing but to throw themselves on the mercy of God, who showed His overflowing goodness in giving His Son to die for them.

However, he did not stop with a general theological discourse. He relentlessly called out the town sins. "How many kinds of wickedness are there?" he asked, and then answered: irreverence in God's house, disregard of the Sabbath, neglect of family prayer, disobedience to parents, quarreling, greediness, sensuality, hatred of one's neighbor. Secret sins were held up for all to see.

The Holy Spirit used the sharp edges of the sermons to cut deep. People couldn't sleep on Sunday nights. The next day they could talk of nothing but the amazing change in the pulpit.

First Conversions

It was in December 1734 that the first conversions came. There were five or six "savingly converted"—among them a young woman who was known as a notorious "company-keeper," a boisterous reveler. The news of her conversion "seemed to be like a flash of lightning upon the hearts of the young people, all over the town, and upon many others."

"Presently upon this," Edwards wrote in his *Narrative of Surprising Conversions*, "a great and earnest concern about the great things of religion and the eternal world became universal in all parts of the town, and among persons of all degrees and all ages; the noise among the dry bones waxed louder and louder; all other talk but about spiritual and eternal things was soon thrown by." He also wrote, "The Spirit of God began extraordinarily to . . . work among us. . . . This work of God, as it was carried on and the number of true saints multiplied, soon made a glorious alteration to the town."

People gathered in their homes to pray. Shops closed up business. The public assemblies were "beautiful, the congregation was alive in God's service, everyone earnestly intent on the public worship, every hearer eager to drink in the words of the minister."

Tears flowed—some weeping in sorrow and distress, others with joy and love, others with pity and concern for the souls of their neighbors. Day and night people came to the parsonage to bring news of their conversion or to seek the pastor's help.

Soon the revival spilled over into other towns. Before long 100 communities were affected. In six months, 300 people were converted in Northampton (population 1,100). One hundred were received in membership before the next Communion.

In May 1735, the revival began to cool off, but it was only a flicker of greater things to come when twenty-five-year-old George Whitefield, a colleague of John and Charles Wesley in England, would burst upon the scene.

Edwards had touched off the revival fire. George Whitefield swept the white-hot flames through all of New England and into the South.

Edwards was the flint; Whitefield the tinder.

Edwards was tall, thin, deliberate. Whitefield, only of average height, jumped about like a jack-in-the-box. Edwards spoke with quiet intensity, his thin tones reaching the dim corners of the balconies. Whitefield hurled Gospel truths like thunderbolts, his eyes flashing (one eye squinted, an aftereffect of the measles).

Edwards' sermons were masterpieces of theological thought. He built truth upon truth until the weight of them bore down on his listeners like a pile driver. Whitefield's sermons, unremarkable from a theological standpoint, had the effect of a red-hot fork thrust into a stick of butter. But they had one thing in common: the conviction that the Gospel compels a personal decision that will change an ordinary man into a new being.

Powerful Preaching

Edwards' peculiar power lay in his ability to paint pictures. His aim was to make heaven and hell, their joys and terrors, as real as if you could point them out in a photo.

In his most famous sermon, "Sinners in the Hands of an Angry God," he compared the sinner with some spider or loathsome insect suspended over the flames. "You hang by a slender thread, with the flames of divine wrath flashing about it, and ready every moment to singe and burn it asunder; and you have nothing to lay hold of to save yourself, nothing to keep off the flames of wrath, nothing of your own, nothing that you have ever done, nothing that you can do, to induce God to spare you one moment."

Unconsciously, people grasped the pews to keep from sliding into the pit. A minister who was in the pulpit grabbed at Edwards' black gown, exclaiming, "Mr. Edwards, Mr. Edwards, is not God a God of mercy?" To be sure, it was not all hellfire and brimstone. He could create equally as vivid pictures of the love and mercy of God and the beauty of heaven.

Whitefield believed in using his voice. "I love those who thunder out the word," he once said. "The Christian world is in a dead sleep. Nothing but a loud voice can awaken them out of it."

His enunciation was faultless. David Garrick, an English actor and playwright, once remarked that if Whitefield were on the stage, he could make an audience weep or tremble by his utterance of the one word *Oh*. Benjamin Franklin, who often heard him preach, stated that "every accent, every emphasis, every modulation of voice was so perfectly tuned and well placed, that without being interested in the subject one could not help being pleased with the discourse."

Whitefield too could paint pictures. One time he compared the sinner with a helpless blind beggar wandering on the edge of a precipice. As he stumbles forward, his staff slips from his hands and falls into the abyss. Unconscious of his danger, he stoops down to recover it. Carried away by the vividness, someone in the listening crowd exclaimed, "He's gone! He's gone!"

Whitefield Arrives

When New England heard that Whitefield was coming, it trembled in anticipation. Sporadic revivals were still in progress, but it seemed that the people were holding their breath for the advent of the young man who had shaken England.

At Philadelphia, his first stop after founding an orphanage in Georgia, Whitefield spoke to thousands from the balcony of the courthouse on Market Street. Every word was distinctly heard, it was said, by seamen on board a ship anchored at the wharf, some 400 feet away.

From 1738 to 1770, he made seven journeys to America, preaching from Georgia to New Hampshire and Maine. In one 75-day period, he preached 175 times and traveled 800 miles. Historian Mark Noll wrote that on the New England preaching circuit in the fall of 1740, "Whitefield addressed crowds of up to eight thousand people nearly every day for over a month. That tour may have been the most sensational event in the history of American religion."

He preached in meetinghouses, in barns, in fields, from wagons. Everywhere it was the same—people convicted of sin, driven to the foot of the cross. At none of the meetings was there an "invitation." Whitefield merely preached and then waited for the Spirit to move. There were no counselors, no decision cards. When people were converted, they leaped up to tell about it or made it known later.

At Whiteclay Creek, New Jersey, several thousand gathered. Whitefield felt moved to sing "with unspeakable comfort" the Twenty-third Psalm. When he got to the line "In presence of my spiteful foes, He does my table spread," "the melting soon began and the power increased more and more, till the greatest part of the congregation was exceedingly moved."

While preaching from a wagon in Basking Ridge, New Jersey, Whitefield noticed a little boy weeping "as though his little heart would break." Whitefield interrupted his sermon and had the boy picked up and put in the wagon. He announced that since old church members would not cry after Christ, the boy would preach to them. God, he said, was displaying His sovereignty, "out of an infant's mouth perfecting praise."

"God so blessed this," Whitefield testified, "that a universal concern fell on the congregation again. Fresh persons dropped down here and there, and the cry increased more and more."

Ministers were among the converts. At dinner with fellow ministers in Stamford, Connecticut, Whitefield spoke forcefully against the practice of sending unconverted persons into the ministry. Two ministers, with tears in their eyes, publicly confessed they laid hands on young men without so much as asking them whether they were born again of God or not. After dinner, one old minister called Whitefield aside. Speaking with difficulty through his tears, he said, "I have been a scholar and have preached the doctrines of grace for a long time. But I believe I have never felt the power of them in my own soul."

Others Take Up the Revival Torch

Other New England ministers took up the revival torch. Notable among them: Theodore Frelinghuysen, Samuel Blair, and Presbyterian William Tennent and his four sons. In 1727, Tennent founded a ministerial school in Warminster, Pennsylvania, derisively called the "Log College" by his opponents, which was the forerunner of Princeton University. Local ministers were also awakening their parishes.

A dramatic incident occurred at Portsmouth, New Hampshire. As an evening meeting was going on, the chimney of the house next door caught fire. When the flames flashed on the windows of the meetinghouse, the cry went up: "Christ is coming to judge us!" People fell down in fear. Even when the cause of the flash was explained, they continued to be alarmed. "If we're so unprepared for judgment that the light of a burning chimney throws us into panic," they said, "how much in need we are of repentance!"

Afterward the minister visited their homes. He found "there was hardly any such thing as entering into a house in which there was not some poor, wounded, and distressed soul." He was called into one house after another.

The people begged him not to leave them until prayer had solemnly been offered on their behalf.

As the revival burned on, strange things began to happen. Some people went into trances and saw visions. They were seized by violent muscular contractions called "the jerks." Laymen began to preach on the spur of the moment, motivated, they said, by "impulses" from the Holy Spirit.

After a sermon in Lyme, Connecticut, "many had their countenances changed; their thoughts seemed to trouble them, so that the joints of their loins were loosed, and their knees smote one against another. Great numbers cried out aloud in the anguish of their souls. Several brave men fell as though a cannon had been discharged and a ball had made its way through their hearts." People had to be carried from the meetinghouse.

At first, ministers hesitated to do anything about the disorders, fearing it might hinder the revival. But eventually it became clear that something would have to be done.

In a sermon called "Needful Caution in a Critical Day," the minister at Lyme told his people to "watch against everything in principle and practice that has a tendency to bring any blemishes upon the work of divine grace." He pointed out that irregular physical actions might in themselves come to be considered of spiritual value. People would seek after them and produce them at will, degrading faith into "mere nervous excitement."

Because of these disorders, which the leaders of the revival were not able to keep in check, opposition to the whole awakening arose. Then, too, evangelists who took to preaching without permission in others' parishes made themselves unpopular to the local ministers.

One evangelist, James Davenport, went from place to place denouncing the New England ministers. They were all unconverted men, he said, leading their flocks blindfolded to hell. He called on the converted to separate themselves from their unconverted brethren. Many did. The separatists denounced the churches as being made up of hypocrites and believed the Gospel could best be preached by uneducated—but converted—lay preachers. Some held that bodily manifestations *must* accompany true conversions. Some laid down rules as to what feelings and experiences a professing Christian *must* describe to be regarded as converted.

Whitefield and Lukewarm Clergy

Whitefield did not actively encourage the separatists. However, he and others did accuse the general clergy of lukewarmness and lack of spirituality. On his second visit to New England in 1744, Harvard and Yale colleges published "testimonies" against him. They accused him of approving of the disorders, causing divisions, and deluding people about the orphanage for which he was collecting funds. (The last charge was proved unfounded.) In June 1745, the General Association of Connecticut voted that it was not "advisable for any of our ministers to admit him to their pulpits or for any of our people to attend his ministrations."

Jonathan Edwards rose up to defend the revival. In two treatises, *The Distinguishing Marks of a Work of the Spirit of God* and *Some Thoughts Concerning the Present Revival of Religion in New England*, he spoke his mind on the emotional displays, taking a middle ground. Though he viewed them with deep concern, at the same time he insisted there might well be a connection between such manifestations and the unusual presence of divine power.

In any case, he argued, we should not judge the revival by these. We should look at the work as a whole, which he was ready to declare was of God. If those who criticize, he said, "wait to see a work of God without difficulties and stumbling blocks, it will be like the fool's waiting at the riverside to have the water all run by."

Later on Edwards had more to say on the subject of the conversion experience. In his *Treatise Concerning Religious Affections*, he reaffirmed his belief that conversion is undeniably an emotional affair. Though the intellect enters in, feeling, not thought, is the gateway to knowing God. He was not concerned by the nature of the outward displays. What counts, he argued, is whether or not they indicate an inner change that will not fade when the first blush of emotional upheaval wears away.

So well did he reason that his treatise has gone down as the chief factor in making sudden spiritual conversion intellectually respectable as well as scripturally sound.

If the separatists hoped for support from Edwards, they were mistaken. He took the wind out of their sails with his treatise on *Qualifications of Full Communion*, which rolled through the Halfway Covenant like a bowling ball. The point of the treatise: the Scriptures do not recognize two kinds of saints. There is but one class—those who profess a "renovation of heart" in addition to knowledge of the doctrine and decent living.

He did not, as the separatists did, say specifically what "inward experiences" must be related. Neither did he say the converted person must necessarily know the time and place of his conversion. Edwards' view was eventually accepted almost without exception by the New England churches.

The controversies did not bog down the revival. In fact, it almost can be said that they were an evidence of it. For they showed that people were stirred. Revival upset the status quo. Things no longer ran smoothly. Satan opposed. And even those used of God were in danger of becoming proud, arrogant, and rash. But Satan could not stop the revival.

The last embers of the Great Awakening did not die out until 1760; the revival had gone on for twenty years. What were the results?

The most obvious result was the ingathering of souls. It is estimated that 25,000 to 50,000 people were added to the New England churches. Since the population of the entire New England colonies at that time was no more than 340,000, the church increased by 8 to 15 percent. It is a matter of record that from 1740 to 1760, 150 new Congregational churches were founded. Separatist churches multiplied, and so did Baptist and Presbyterian churches.

And there were other immediate results: The awakening killed the idea (at least for a century) that an unconverted ministry might be tolerated. It greatly advanced the cause of ministerial education as well as education in general. It advanced the cause of missions among the Native Americans. It struck a blow for the cause of religious liberty (the Great Awakening undoubtedly spurred First Amendment support for religious liberty). It made the ministries of traveling evangelists not only respectable but desirable.

The Verdict of History

What is the verdict after almost three centuries have gone by?

One biographer of Jonathan Edwards terms the Great Awakening "the most potent, constructive force in American life during the mid-century." Through it, God undoubtedly fortified the church against the onslaught of skepticism and rationalism soon to come from Europe. Historians disagree on what effect it had on stabilizing the colonies so that they could present a united front to Great Britain in the coming Revolution. But it is certain that the Awakening had a part to play in cementing Christian principles into the foundation of American government.

Most importantly, the Great Awakening revitalized the spiritual experience of the average man. Christianity once again became personal and important to him. With a clarity that staggered him, he saw that a man cannot be saved without experiencing the new birth through Jesus Christ.

The Great Awakening defeated the enemies of spiritual indifference and theological fuzziness that threatened Christianity in the New World. But after the Revolution, Christianity was challenged by an entirely different enemy. How God moved to defeat this adversary is the story of the next great American revival, the Revival of 1800.

two

Revival Transforms the Frontier

On a bleak wintry day in 1794, twenty-three New England ministers sat down together to consider a problem that was pressing heavily upon them. They were disturbed about the spiritual condition of their country.

Here was the situation: The effects of the Great Awakening of 1735 had worn off. The seeds of aggressive antireligious teachings such as natural philosophy, imported from revolutionary France and watered by such men as Thomas Paine, were yielding their poisonous fruit.

Eastern colleges were rife with the skepticism of the age. Lawlessness ruled on the Western frontier. People were floundering in the bog of confusion created by the French and Indian War and the Revolution. The established churches, most of which had sided with England in the struggle for independence, had lost their influence, and there were few praying people.

The ministers were agreed on one thing—a revival was desperately needed.

"What shall we do about it?" they asked themselves. The only answer: pray.

They issued a "circular letter" calling on church people to pray for revival. They were specific. Let there be "public prayer and praise, accompanied with such instruction from God's Word, as might be judged proper, on every first Tuesday of the four quarters of the year, beginning with the first Tuesday of January 1795, at two o'clock in the afternoon . . . and so continuing from quarter to quarter, and from year to year, until, the good providence of God prospering our endeavors, we shall obtain the blessing for which we pray."

Apparently hearts were hungry, for there was an enthusiastic response.

All over the country, little praying bands sprang up. In the West (Ohio, Kentucky, Tennessee), "covenants" were entered into by Christian people to spend a whole day each month in prayer plus a half hour every Saturday night and every Sunday morning.

Seminary students met to study the history of revivals. Church members formed "Aaron and Hur Societies" to "hold up the hands" of their ministers through intercession. Groups of young men went to their knees to pray for other young men. Parents prayed for their children's conversion.

The stage was set. What happened as a result of this concerted prayer effort has gone down as the most far-reaching revival to this point in American history.

Sparks Become Flames

Of course it didn't happen all at once. As far back as 1790, towns here and there were ignited by the spark of revival. But it wasn't until people began praying determinedly that the sparks became white-hot flames.

How did these revivals start? Dr. Edward D. Griffin, later president of Williams College, tells the story of the beginning of revival in New Hartford, Connecticut, in 1795 and how it continued.

"On the fourth of November [1795]," he wrote, "I went to the house of God saying, 'My soul, wait thou only, only, *only* upon God, for my expectation is from Him.' During the morning I scarcely looked at the audience and cared not whether they were asleep or awake, feeling that the question of a revival did not lie between me and them, but was to be settled in heaven."

The essence of Griffin's message: "Jesus of Nazareth was passing by, and we were left and could hardly hope for another visit so soon, and the awful prospects for sinners in the middle of life, if another revival should not come in twelve or fifteen years. I seemed to take eternal leave of families out of Christ," said he. "I came near falling. I thought I should be obliged to stop, but I was carried through."

The next day it was apparent that a revival had come. A dozen families were under conviction. In the course of the winter and the next year about 100 were "hopefully added to the Lord."

Griffin wrote in 1839: "Revivals have never ceased since then."

Dancing Turns to Tears

In 1799, two young men in Granville, Massachusetts, were suddenly taken violently ill at a dance and had to be carried out. One of them died, but not before he had told his weeping mother, "Oh, I cannot die; I am unprepared!" A woman who had attended the same dance became sick, and in a short time she too was near death.

The young people of the town were naturally sobered by these events. When the minister, Timothy M. Cooley, invited them to his study, they came willingly and listened attentively when he told them the "one thing needful." Later at a social gathering, someone took out a violin and began to play it. This was usually the signal for an evening of fun and dancing. But instead, many broke down in tears. It wasn't long until conversions came—and a revival.

The revival in New England was solemn and orderly. There were tears of repentance and joy, but no spectacular events. For instance, a pastor in Andover, Massachusetts, decided to hold classes for the young people of the town. They were given theological questions to answer. Afterward their papers were read without anyone knowing who wrote what. The students began to think seriously of their souls. It was not long before several were converted, touching off a revival that lasted for eighteen months. A strange way for a revival to begin, perhaps, but that was the way it was.

There was no single leader towering head and shoulders above others as did Jonathan Edwards in the Great Awakening. Instead, there were many leaders. To be sure, they were not prominent men in the sense that their names were on everyone's lips. Sometimes their influence was limited to a single village. But they were important men in the sight of God.

Take Jeremiah Hallock. As a boy he "neither saw nor heard of awakenings," and "conviction, conversion, and revivals were terms with which I was unacquainted." But in 1779, when he was twenty-one, something happened to him. While he was at work alone, he was "impressed with a sense of his dependence on God" and "of the sinfulness of his heart." He afterward wrote, "The law of God appeared just, and I saw myself a sinner, and Christ and the way of salvation by Him looked pleasant."

Soon he was called to military duty in the Revolutionary War. He entered a barn with his fellow soldiers and "found myself surrounded by my young companions, exhorting them on the subject of religion." Hallock was surprised to find himself in the middle of revival. Since there was no clergyman, Hallock was often called upon to lead the meetings. In a few months he entered ministerial training, and in 1785, he became a pastor at West Simsbury, Connecticut, not far from New Hartford, where Edward Griffin was pastor. The two met together often to pray for a lasting revival.

In 1798, revival came. But after a few weeks it showed signs of dying out as meeting attendance fell off. Hallock said, "We were greatly afraid that all was about to decline and die. This was indeed a trying hour. No fond parent ever watched the fever of his child at the hour of its crisis with more anxious and interested feelings than numbers of God's praying friends watched the work of the Spirit at this critical moment. The thoughts of its going off were more dreadful than the grave." His concern was rewarded. The meetinghouse was filled night after night. In a few days Hallock counted sixty or seventy converts.

Not only were towns turned upside down in the Revival of 1800, but the colleges—where America's future leaders were being trained—did an about-face.

Yale Shaken

At Yale College, a revival "shook the institution to its center." God's instrument here was Timothy Dwight, a grandson of Jonathan Edwards. Yale was such a hotbed of "infidelity" and antireligious sentiment that the students called one another by the names of Voltaire, Rousseau, and other French intellectuals.

Dwight became president in 1795. He met the situation head on. The students handed him a list of subjects for class debate, thinking to prove that free discussion was limited at Yale. To their surprise, Dwight chose the subject "Is the Bible the Word of God?" He told the students to do their best. Most of the students took the side of infidelity. But when the debate was over, Dwight's review of their arguments convinced them they really didn't know what they were talking about. Dwight then preached a famous series of sermons in the college chapel. Most shattering was his 1796 baccalaureate sermon called "The Nature and Danger of Infidel Philosophy." The effect was immediate. "From that moment infidelity was not only without a stronghold," wrote a student, "but without a lurking place. To espouse her cause was now as unpopular as before it had been to profess a belief in Christianity."

That same year, twenty-six Yale students founded the Moral Society of Yale College. It discouraged profanity, immorality, and excessive drinking. By 1800, the society included "between one-third and one-half of all the students [at Yale] in its membership." Its influence laid the foundation for four revivals at Yale in the opening decades of the nineteenth century.

Revival in the West

While New England society was being revolutionized through revival, the settlements of the West were being awakened by a revival totally different in nature. The newly developing American character molded the revival into a new shape. With its boisterous, demonstrative, almost primitive spirit, it was uniquely American.

The story of the revival in the West is the story of the camp meeting and of the itinerant, semi-educated backwoods circuit rider associated with it.

Among the band of earnest young men who set out to reclaim the backwoods for God was James McGready. Born in Pennsylvania around 1760 of Scotch-Irish parents, McGready was such a good little boy that he caught his uncle's eye. His uncle knew just the place for him—the seminary. So when he grew up, McGready was trained as a Presbyterian minister.

Then one day he got a rude awakening. He accidentally overheard two friends talking about him. The gist of what they said was this: Though McGready was a minister in the Presbyterian church, he was merely following the formal rules and was actually a stranger to regenerating grace. McGready was stunned and hurt at first. Then he looked into his heart and found the answer there. He had had no experience of the inward work of God's grace on his life.

Night after night, McGready prayed for the experience of the new birth. An examination of Scripture convinced him that he must have it. He found the new spiritual life he was seeking at a meeting near the Monongahela River. This new experience transformed his life. He decided that his life mission would be to awaken others and lead them to the spiritual life he had found.

McGready set out to preach in the Carolinas in 1788. But he stirred up the people so much that he was accused of "running people distracted." His life was threatened in a letter written in blood. His pulpit was burned down.

Revival Takes Root

Because of opposition, McGready went west to Kentucky in 1796, becoming pastor of three churches in Logan County. This section was known as Rogue's Harbor because of the fugitives from justice who hid out there. It was in those churches that the revival took root.

In 1797, a woman in one of McGready's churches became convicted of her sin and was soon after "filled with joy and peace in believing." The transformation in her life sparked a revival that saw "men under deep conviction spending days alone in the woods weeping and praying."

In July 1799, Communion was administered at Mc-Gready's church at Red River, Kentucky. While Mc-Gready preached, some of the most "bold, daring" sinners of the region broke down like babies. After the meeting was over, people lingered on, praying.

A meeting was held at Red River in June 1800 with perhaps 500 people attending. It was a forerunner of things to come. Two fellow churchmen, William Hodges and John Bankin, aided McGready. John and William McGee, visitors from Tennessee, were on hand as observers.

The meetings began on a Friday and were scheduled to continue through Monday. During the first two days, the congregation melted into tears several times. When the Lord's Supper was observed on Sunday, William Hodges' sermon caused one woman to scream loudly. Others dropped to the floor crying, "What shall I do to be saved?"

The official meeting over, three of the ministers left the church. But no one in the congregation moved. They sat rapt in silence. The McGee brothers had remained behind. Suddenly William McGee sank down on the floor of the pulpit. At the same time, John was seized by a violent trembling but, pulling himself together, managed to make one final appeal. He exhorted the people to "let the Lord Omnipotent reign in their hearts and submit to Him."

The woman who had screamed under Hodges' preaching earlier "shouted tremendously." John McGee left the pulpit to attend to her. Several bystanders told him, "You know, these Presbyterians are much for order. They'll not bear this confusion. Go back and be quiet." McGee started to turn back, then something stopped him. Feeling he was witnessing the work of God, he went through the house shouting and exhorting with "all possible ecstasy and energy." In no time at all "the floor was covered with the slain [in the spirit]."

The news spread like a wildfire. Some people were disgusted. Most were captivated. When they heard that McGready was planning another Communion service at Gasper River, most people couldn't wait to get there. This famous meeting was probably the first planned camp meeting.

Woodsmen set about clearing away underbrush and building a preaching stand outside the tiny church. Simple log seats were arranged. Thirteen wagons were brought to the meetinghouse loaded with people and provisions. Some people traveled 100 miles to get there. The meeting began on Saturday evening and lasted until Tuesday morning.

"Ready to Faint or Die for Christ"

After the formal indoor services were over on the first night, groups of "seriously exercised Christians" gathered around the grounds. Most of the ministers and several hundred worshipers remained at the meetinghouse all night. People struggled in the pangs of the new birth, "ready to faint or die for Christ, almost upon the brink of desperation." Others began to tell of "the sweet wonders" they saw in Christ. Everywhere ministers and experienced Christians prayed with inquiring souls. The meeting continued until daybreak. At the close of John McGee's sermon on Sunday, "the power of God seemed to shake the whole assembly."

This was the beginning of camp meeting after camp meeting. In August of the same year, a meeting was held at Muddy River. There were twenty-two wagons loaded with people and their provisions. People came expecting to camp out for four to six days.

One of those who was impressed by the Logan County meetings was Barton W. Stone. He was serving two congregations in Concord and Cane Ridge in Bourbon County, clear across the state of Kentucky. He returned home and told his people what he had seen. Soon after—in August 1801—Cane Ridge was the scene of what many people regard as the most spectacular of the revival meetings of the 1800 revival.

It was probably the largest revival meeting ever held in early-day America and the most disorderly and electrifying. Attendance estimates range from 10,000 to 25,000. People of all denominations came.

An eyewitness described the scene: "The roads were crowded with wagons, carriages, horses, and footmen moving to the solemn camp. . . . It was judged by military men on the ground that between twenty and thirty thousand persons were assembled. Four or five preachers spoke at the same time in different parts of the encampment without confusion. The Methodist and Baptist preachers aided in the work and all appeared cordially united in it. They were of one mind and soul;

the salvation of sinners was the one object. They all engaged in singing the same songs, all united in prayer, all preached the same things."

One eyewitness reported that some 800 persons "were struck down," lying unresponsive for anywhere from fifteen minutes to six, eight, or ten hours.

James Finley, later a circuit rider, dated his conversion from this meeting. He described the sound as "like the roar of Niagara." At one time he saw at least 500 swept down in a moment with shrieks and shouts.

"Stand Still and See"

At a Presbyterian meeting held at Cross Roads Church in Orange County, the pastor rose to dismiss the service. He was disappointed that there had been no evidence of revival. He tried to speak, but, overcome by emotion, sat down without saying a word. He got up again, but still was unable to go on. Suddenly a young man visiting from Tennessee, where the revival was already making headway, raised both hands and with a loud voice exclaimed, "Stand still and see the salvation of God!" The congregation was electrified. Many people fell to the ground.

Of course some people opposed the revival, as they always will. But many of the most violently opposed came under its influence. A deist in the neighborhood of Cane Ridge at the beginning of the revival told Barton Stone, "I always thought before, you were an honest man; but now I am convinced you are deceiving the people." Stone reported, "I viewed him with pity and mildly spoke a few words to him. Immediately he fell as a dead man and rose no more until he confessed the error of his ways."

The revival preaching was spectacular. The lot of the sinner was painted in vivid colors. One of James McGready's sermons was on the text, "The fool hath said in his heart, There is no God" (Psalm 14:1 KJV). He spoke of the "black, flaming vultures of hell encircling the fool at death, the fiends dragging him into the eternal gulf as he roars and screams and yells while accursed sinners of Tyre and Sidon and Sodom and Gomorrah" spring to the right and left and make way for him to pass. Finally he sinks to the deepest cavern in the flaming abyss where "his consciousness like a never-dying worm stings him and forever gnaws his soul."

It was the hardened sinner indeed who could ignore such preaching.

On one occasion, Peter Cartwright, the famed Methodist circuit rider, who had a great sense of humor, spent some forty minutes on "waggish talk" in which "shafts of ridicule, bon mots, puns and side-splitting anecdotes sparkled, flashed and flew like hail, till the vast auditory was convulsed with laughter." Then his manner changed. His face grew serious, his voice earnest. Soon "tears came to his eyes and he descanted on the horrors of hell till every shuddering face was turned downward, as if expecting to see the solid globe rent asunder."

Physical Manifestations

A feature of the revival in the West, though not in New England, was the physical manifestations. These were seen at the time of the Great Awakening, but they reached a higher pitch in the Revival of 1800.

Of the manifestations, the "falling exercise" was the most common. According to one chronicler, this is what usually happened: "When a person begins to be affected, he generally sinks down in the place where he stood and is for a few minutes overwhelmed in tears. He then makes a weeping noise. Then his voice becomes feeble, his features composed. Finally, he is motionless and speechless. During this time his pulse is slow, his hands and feet are cold, the skin 'fresh and clear,' the eyes partly closed. Speech and motion return gradually. When 'faith is obtained,' the person rises up and shouts 'glory to God,' remaining in a state of ecstasy."

A person with "the jerks" was also a familiar sight at the camp meetings. Sometimes just the head would jerk back and forth, from side to side; sometimes the whole body. Peter Cartwright recollected that he had seen more than 500 persons jerking at one time.

Then there were the "rolling exercises" (people would roll over and over like a wheel), the "dancing exercise" (when the jerking of legs looked like dancing), and the "running exercises" (merely an attempt to "run away" from the physical manifestations).

Perhaps the most peculiar of all was the "barking exercise." Men "went down on all fours and barked until they grew hoarse." Actually the barks probably were grunts resulting from the suddenness of the jerks. The name originated when an old Presbyterian clergyman got the jerks and grasped a tree for support. Some punster saw him and reported he had found the minister "barking up a tree."

Naturally the curious and scornful were attracted by such goings on. One man brought a pole with a sharp needle in the end to poke those who fell. To his surprise, he fell down himself and was speechless for an hour. When he recovered, he confessed the trick he had intended playing.

Certainly the Revival of 1800 displayed more phys ical manifestations than any other revival in history. They seemed to be an integral part of the awakening. Almost weird to Americans today, these physical reactions have been criticized more often than any other phase of the Revival of 1800.

Evangelicals can draw three general conclusions:

1. When God moves the spirit of man, He also touches his emotions. Some men are moved more intensely than others. Certainly, in the Bible, King Saul prophesied, David danced, and Saul (later Paul) fell blinded when the Spirit of God came upon him. No doubt, many of the physical manifestations of the Revival of 1800 were of God.

2. Satan is a master counterfeiter. Even as he tries to counterfeit conversion, he tries to counterfeit

its emotional reaction. And he was busy during the camp meetings of 1800 to degrade them by emotional excesses.

3. Modern psychology explains many such reactions in terms of group behavior. Probably some of the manifestations were natural in the highly emotional surroundings. In fact, God may have used some of these natural reactions to attract the attention of the spiritually hardened pioneers.

Probably a combination of these three explanations would best describe the physical reactions of the Revival of 1800.

Preachers Join Hands

Certainly it is clear that Christians afraid of emotion, afraid of revealing their hidden sins and pride in public, are not those whom God will choose to start a revival. And the Revival of 1800 was definitely a revival of Christians. The conversion of people outside the church came only after the churches were revitalized.

The core of the camp meeting revivals was the altar service. Usually the "mourners' bench" was directly in front of the pulpit. To the godly, this structure was known as the "altar"; to scoffers, it was "the pen." By the 1820s, the term "anxious seat" came into use. Sometimes the altar was merely a row of seats. Or it could be a spacious enclosed area, often twenty or thirty feet square, down the center of which ran a rail fence segregating men from women. It was here that sinners who wished to be instructed came to pray.

"Praying circles" or "prayer rings" materialized when a group of respected laymen and preachers joined hands to form a circle and asked all who felt themselves in need of prayer to enter it.

Results of the Revival of 1800

The revival lasted well into the nineteenth century. Presbyterians started the revival, but it was Baptists and especially the Methodists—men such as Francis Asbury and Peter Cartwright—who carried it forward.

During the main revival period, the Methodists could boast an average yearly increase of 2,000 members. The Methodist Western Conference had a membership of 2,700 before the revival; after the revival, the number had leaped to 12,000. In Kentucky, an estimated 10,000 were added to the Baptist churches from 1799 to 1803. The Presbyterians also gained, though later schisms were responsible for that church losing ground in the West.

The Cumberland Presbyterian Church was formed by Barton W. Stone and others. This split was the result of a softening of their ideas on the Calvinistic doctrine of predestination. In contrast to the emphasis on divine sovereignty in the Great Awakening, the central doctrine of the Revival of 1800 was human responsibility and duty.

Another new group coming out of the revival was the Campbellites (now called the Disciples of Christ). They formed as a protest against organized religion, professing to pattern their congregations on the New Testament standard. That is why they called themselves simply "Christians."

Aside from the numerical additions to the churches, what were the results of the revival? There were many.

The Revival of 1800 put the toddling baby nation solidly on its feet. It stabilized the West. During the revival, travelers in Kentucky found the people "as remarkable for sobriety as they had formerly been for dissolution and immorality." Kentucky, one traveler said, was "the most moral place I had ever seen." As pioneers moved farther west, they were heavily populated with sound Christians. The church became a major factor in the fight against lawlessness, and eventually it triumphed.

One of the proudest achievements of the Revival of 1800 was the impetus it gave to missions. In the shelter of a haystack during a storm in August 1806, a number of students at Williams College in Williamstown, Massachusetts, which underwent a great revival, pledged themselves to lives of work for the kingdom of God. The outcome was the formation of the American Board of Commissioners for Foreign Missions. For twenty-seven years this was the agency that backed all Congregational, Presbyterian, Dutch Reformed, and German Reformed missionaries. Another result of the Haystack Prayer Meeting was the formation of the American Bible Society.

The Sunday school movement in the United States got a tremendous push from the revival. The first Sunday School Union was formed in Philadelphia in 1791. It was the forerunner of the American Sunday School Union, started in 1824.

Antislavery sentiment sprouted during the revival. Barton W. Stone emancipated his slaves during the period. In 1818, the General Association of the Presbyterian Church called slavery "a gross violation of the most precious and sacred rights of human nature; as utterly inconsistent with the law of God."

The revival came at a time when the churches were just getting used to the idea of the disestablishment—separation from the state. The preaching of the freedom of the Gospel and the healthy influence of the revival put starch into their backs and made them able to stand alone.

Like the Great Awakening, this revival demonstrated that a revival cannot be pushed, pulled, and molded into any prearranged shape. Men were the instruments, but any time they tried to restrict the revival, they found themselves swept aside. In 1800 as in 1735, those who opposed the revival eventually came around to accepting its fruits as readily as those who backed it.

By the 1830s and 1840s, vocal resistance among Christians had all but died out. In fact, when by 1845 the revival fire had been doused by the rise of a national crisis, it was a matter of great concern among all church people.

The Great Awakening of 1735 had successfully dealt with the disease of spiritual indifference. The Revival of 1800 had triumphed over infidelity and skepticism. In 1845, an adolescent nation bitterly divided on the issue of slavery desperately needed a renewal of spiritual strength to carry it through the conflict soon to come. In 1857, God met that need through another mighty moving of the Holy Spirit.

three

Revival Born
in a Prayer Meeting

It was exactly 12 noon on September 23, 1857. A tall, middle-aged former businessman climbed creaking stairs to the third story of an old church building in the heart of lower New York City. He entered an empty room, pulled out his pocket watch, and sat down to wait. The sign outside read "Prayer Meeting from 12 to 1 o'clock—Stop 5, 10, or 20 minutes, or the whole hour, as your time admits." It looked as though no one cared or had the time. As the minutes ticked by, the solitary waiter wondered if it were all a mistake.

For some three months he had been visiting boardinghouses, shops, and offices, inviting people to the eighty-eight-year-old Old Dutch North Church at Fulton and Williams streets. The church had fallen on hard times. Old families had moved away. The business neighborhood was teeming with an ever-changing population of immigrants and laborers.

Other churches had left the neighborhood. Many thought that Old Dutch should throw in the towel. But the trustees determined on a last-ditch stand. They decided to hire a lay missionary to conduct a visitation program. The man they picked was Jeremiah Lanphier, a merchant who had no experience whatsoever in church visitation work. At forty-nine years old, Lanphier gave up his trade position to knock on doors for a salary of less than $1,000 a year.

The going was slow. A few new families came, but often Lanphier returned to his room in the evening weary and discouraged. At such time he "spread out his sorrows before the Lord," and he never failed to draw new strength from his time of prayer.

While going on his rounds of visitation, the idea occurred to him that businessmen might like to get away for a short period of prayer once a week while offices were closed for the noon hour. With the permission of church officials, Lanphier passed out flyers and put up the sign. When the day of the first meeting came, he was the only one on hand for it.

Six Come to Pray

He waited ten minutes, then ten more. The minute hand of his watch pointed to 12:30 when at last he heard a step on the creaking stairs. One man came in, then another and another until there were six. After a few minutes of prayer, the meeting was dismissed with the decision that another meeting would be held the following Wednesday.

That small meeting was in no way extraordinary. There was no great outpouring of the Spirit of God. Lanphier had no way of knowing that it was the beginning of a great national revival that would sweep an estimated 1 million people into the kingdom of God.

Looking back, historians can see that conditions were ripe for revival. The Revival of 1800 began a golden age of spiritual interest. But by 1843, a nation intent upon getting and spending had lost interest in religion. The West had opened up. Gold was discovered in California. Railroad building was a craze. The slavery issue was hot. Fortunes ballooned. Faith diminished.

Lanphier did not know much about such things. All he knew was that men stood in need of prayer.

Twenty men came to his second noon-hour meeting. The following Wednesday, forty. Lanphier decided to make the meeting a daily event in a larger room.

That very week—on October 14, 1857—the nation was staggered by the worst financial panic in its history and the first worldwide economic crisis. Banks closed, businesses failed, men were out of work, families went hungry.

The "Panic of 1857," no doubt, had something to do with the astonishing growth of Lanphier's noon meeting (by now called "the Fulton Street Prayer Meeting"). In a short time the meeting had taken over the whole building with crowds of more than 3,000. Lawyers and physicians, merchants and clerks, bankers and brokers, manufacturers and mechanics, concierges and messenger boys—all came. Wagon drivers would drive up to the curb, tie up their horses, and come in for a few minutes of prayer.

Rules were drawn up. Signs were posted. One read "Brethren are earnestly requested to adhere to the 5-minute rule." Another: "Prayers and exhortations not to exceed 5 minutes, in order to give all an opportunity."

It seemed that the Fulton Street Prayer Meeting had touched a nerve. The revival-prayer impulse flashed from coast to coast.

On November 5, 1857, a New York newspaper carried the story of a revival in Hamilton, Ontario, Canada, in which 300 to 400 people were converted in a few days. Accounts of local revivals began to appear in papers in November. And in December, a three-day

Presbyterian convention was held at Pittsburgh to consider the necessity for a general revival. Shortly thereafter a similar one was called in Cincinnati.

New York Bows in Prayer

Within six months, 10,000 businessmen (out of a population of 800,000) were gathering *daily* in New York City for prayer. In January 1858, there were at least twenty other prayer meetings going full tilt in the city. Many of them were sparked by the Young Men's Christian Association (YMCA). Other cities had them too.

By January 1858, newspapers were sending reporters to cover the meetings. "The Progress of the Revival" became a standing news headline. Remarkable cases of awakening were detailed at length, and there were many.

One time a man wandered into the Fulton Street meeting who intended to murder a woman and then commit suicide. He listened as someone was delivering a fervent appeal for conversion and urging the duty of repentance. Suddenly the would-be murderer startled everyone by crying out, "Oh! What shall I do to be saved!" Just then another man arose, and with tears streaming down his cheeks asked the meeting to sing the hymn "Rock of Ages, Cleft for Me." At the conclusion of the service, both men were converted.

Another time an aged pastor got up to pray for the son of another clergyman. Unknown to him, his own son was sitting some distance behind him. The young man, knowing himself to be a sinner, was so impressed at hearing his father pray for another man's son that he made himself known to the meeting and said he wanted to give his heart to God. He became a regular attender at the prayer meeting.

A prizefighter nicknamed "Awful Gardiner" was a prayer-meeting convert. He visited his old friends at Sing Sing Prison and gave his testimony. Among those who were converted was a noted river thief, Jerry McAuley, who later founded the Water Street Mission, one of the first missions for down-and-outs.

On March 17, Burton's Theater on Chambers Street was opened for a noonday prayer meeting. Half an hour before the first service was to begin, the 3,000-seat theater was packed from the musicians' pit to the roof.

By the summer of 1858, news of the prayer meeting had crossed the Atlantic. In August, two Presbyterian ministers from Ireland came to see what it was all about. "We have connected with our synod 500 churches and congregations," they said. "And we have a strong desire that the same gracious dispensation that has blessed you here be bestowed upon all our churches at home." They asked for the prayers of the Fulton Street Prayer Meeting.

Revival Hits Front Pages

For the first time, modern means of communication spread revival news. Prayer meetings exchanged telegraph messages. Newspaper coverage and printed propaganda made it nearly impossible for anyone not to know about the revival. One man who came to the Fulton Street Prayer Meeting said he had been given a flyer advertising the meeting six months before while standing 1,000 miles away on the west bank of the Mississippi River.

But mostly, the revival spread by means of people with changed lives.

One of the six men at the first Fulton Street meeting was a twenty-one-year-old Philadelphian. *Why not a prayer meeting in Philadelphia?* he thought. He and some of his fellow members of the YMCA asked for permission to hold a meeting in the Methodist Episcopal Union Church. The start was dismal. Only about forty came. The meeting was moved to another building more centrally located. Still the crowd stayed around sixty. But suddenly there was a change. On March 8, 1858, about 300 people were present. Two days later, 2,500 people jammed into a larger auditorium. Seats were set up on the stage. After that, no fewer than 3,000 people attended the meeting every day. In May, a tent was put up. Within four months, 150,000 people had prayed in the tent.

Meetings sprang up in other parts of the city. It is estimated that there were 10,000 conversions in Philadelphia in 1858. One denomination received 3,000 new members.

In Boston, where evangelist Charles G. Finney was preaching, a prayer meeting was held in historic Old South Church and in Park Street Church. At least 150 Massachusetts towns were moved by the revival, with 5,000 conversions before the end of March. The Boston correspondent of a Washington newspaper wrote that religion was the chief concern in many cities and towns of New England.

Newspapers everywhere thought the revival was front-page news. Headlines similar to these might have told the story:

New Haven, Connecticut—"City's Biggest Church Packed Twice Daily for Prayer."

Bethel, Connecticut—"Business Shuts Down for Hour Each Day; Everybody Prays."

Albany, New York—"State Legislators Get Down on Knees."

Schenectady, New York—"Ice on the Mohawk River Broken for Baptisms."

Newark, New York—"Firemen's Meeting Attracts 2,000."

Washington, DC—"Five Prayer Meetings Go Round the Clock."

New Haven, Connecticut—"Revival Sweeps Yale."

Early in 1858, the revival power poured over the Appalachian Mountains and into the West. Every major town fell before it—Cleveland, Cincinnati, Detroit, Indianapolis, Minneapolis, Chicago, St. Louis, Omaha—and on to the Pacific Coast.

Eyewitness Describes Meeting

The Fulton Street Prayer Meeting may well be the model for effective prayer meetings today. How were the meetings conducted? Why did they have such power? Fortunately, an eyewitness account, published in 1858, has come down to us:

We take our seat in the middle room, ten minutes before 12 o'clock. A few ladies are seated in one corner, and a few businessmen are scattered here and there through the room. Five minutes to 12, the room begins to fill up rapidly. Two minutes to 12, the leader enters and takes his seat in the desk or pulpit. At 12, punctual to the moment, at the first stroke of the clock the leader arises and commences the meeting by reading two or three verses of the hymn,

> Salvation, oh the joyful sound,
> 'Tis pleasure to our ears;
> A sovereign balm for every wound,
> A cordial for our fears.

Each person finds a hymnbook in his seat; all sing with heart and voice. The leader offers a prayer—short, pointed, to the purpose—then reads a brief portion of Scripture. Ten minutes are now gone. Meantime, requests in sealed envelopes have been going up to the desk for prayer.

A deep, solemn silence settles down upon our meeting. It is holy ground. The leader stands with slips of paper in his hand. He says: "This meeting is now open for prayer. Brethren from a distance are specially invited to take part. All will observe the rules."

All is now breathless attention. A tender solicitude spreads over all those upturned faces. The chairman reads: "A son in North Carolina desires the fervent, effectual prayers of the righteous of this congregation for the immediate conversion of his mother in Connecticut."

In an instant a father rises: "I wish to ask the prayers of this meeting for two sons and a daughter." He sits down and bursts into tears, lays his head down on the railing of the seat before him, and sobs like a broken-hearted child.

A few remarks follow—very brief. The chairman rises with slips of paper in his hand and reads: "A praying sister requests prayers for two unconverted brothers in the city of Detroit; that they be converted and become the true followers of the Lord Jesus Christ."

Another, "Prayers are requested by the people of God for a young man, once a professor of faith, but now a wanderer and going astray."

Two prayers in succession followed these requests— very fervent, very earnest. And others, who rose to pray at the same time, sat down again when they found themselves preceded by the voices already engaged in prayer.

Then arose from all hearts that beautiful hymn, sung with touching pathos, so appropriate too, just in this stage of this meeting with all these cases full before us,

> There is a fountain filled with blood
> Drawn from Immanuel's veins,
> And sinners plunged beneath that flood
> Lose all their guilty stains.

Then followed prayer by one who prays earnestly for all who have been prayed for, for all sinners present, for the perishing thousands in this city, for the spread of revivals all over the land and world.

It is now a quarter to one o'clock. Time has fled on silver wings. . . .

There arose a sailor, now one no more, by reason of ill health, but daily laboring for sailors. He was converted on board a man-of-war, and he knew how hard it was for the converted sailor to stand up firm against the storm of jeers, and reproaches, and taunts of a ship's crew. "Now I am here," he said, "to represent one who has requested me to ask your prayers for a converted sailor this day gone to sea. I parted from him a little time ago, and his fear is, his great fear, that he may dishonor the cause of the blessed Redeemer. Will you pray for this sailor?" Prayer was offered for his keeping and guidance.

Then came the closing hymn, the benediction, and the parting for twenty-three hours.

Chicago Stirred

In Chicago, where 2,000 showed up for prayer in the Metropolitan Theater, a newspaper commented, "So far as the effects of the present religious movement are concerned, they are apparent to all. They are to be seen in every walk of life, to be felt in every phase of society. The merchant, the farmer, the mechanic—all who have been within their influence—have been incited to better things; to a more orderly and honest way of life. All have been more or less influenced by this excitement."

And everywhere, it was a revival of prayer. There was no emotional excess, no unusual disturbances. Just prayer.

Charles Finney said, "There is such a general confidence in the prevalence of prayer that the people very extensively seemed to prefer meeting for prayer to meeting for preaching. The general impression seemed to be, 'We have had instruction until we are hardened; it is time for us to pray.'"

In a church in the Midwest, twenty-five women got together once a week to pray for their unconverted husbands. The pastor traveled to the Fulton Street Prayer Meeting to testify that on the Sunday he had left, the last of the twenty-five husbands had been received into the church.

At the very first union prayer meeting held in Kalamazoo, Michigan, someone put in this request: "A praying wife requests the prayers of this meeting for her unconverted husband, that he may be converted and made an humble disciple of the Lord Jesus." At once a stout, burly man arose and said, "I am that man. I have a praying wife, and this request must be for me. I want you to pray for me." As soon as he sat down, another man got up and said, "*I* am that man. I have a praying wife. She prays for me. And now she asked you to pray for me. I am sure I am that man, and I want you to pray for me." Three, four, or five more arose and said, "We want you to pray for us too." That started a revival that brought at least 500 conversions.

Requests for prayer came to the Fulton Street Prayer Meeting from all parts of the country and Europe. Some were addressed to New York's mayor, who forwarded them to the meeting. A ledger was filled with the requests, such as this: "For pity's sake, lend me your prayers for a firstborn son. He curses me, his widowed mother; and, with a demon scowl, has turned his back on me for life. . . . For God's sake, pray for

Willie that he may be a minister of Christ. For this I dedicated him before his eyes opened on this sinful world."

And this: "The prayers of the Christians of the Fulton Street meeting are earnestly implored by a young lady who has been once a backslider from God, and who, in the midst of peculiarly harassing temptations, is now endeavoring to return fully to her former rest. Do not—*do not* forget her."

And this: "I am a little girl and scarcely know how to write to a perfect stranger on so important a subject. But oh! I want to be a Christian so much; and I have been asking God for a long time to make me one, but He has not answered my prayer yet . . . I am afraid that I have not asked Him in the right way."

Prayer Requests Flood In

These earnest requests weighed deeply on those who attended the Fulton Street Prayer Meeting. Some feared that "a kind of superstitious feeling might be encouraged in those who send these communications and a sense of self-complacency be engendered in those who received them." They feared that the meeting would be seen as *the* meeting, the panacea for all spiritual troubles. However, it was decided that no request could be refused. All they could do was to pray in humility. A flood of letters proved that many of their prayers were answered.

The revival rolled on into 1859 and 1860. There is no telling how long it might have lasted if the Civil War had not broken out. Some writers say that it carried right through the war. It was maintained that 150,000 Confederate soldiers were converted and that at war's end more than one-third of the officers and soldiers of the Confederate Army were professing Christians.

There is disagreement on how far the revival penetrated the South. A Methodist bishop reported that the Southern Methodists gained over 43,000 members as a result of the revival.

When the revival was at high tide through the nation, it was judged that 50,000 persons a week were converted. And the number who joined the churches in 1858 amounted to almost 10 percent of the country's total church membership! If the estimate of 1 million converts is correct (some say the number is closer to 300,000), that accounts for one-thirtieth of the total United States population of that time—and almost all in one year! The revival also had repercussions in the awakening that swept the British Isles.

Statistically, the greatest gainers were the Methodist churches. In 1858, the northern churches received over 135,000 new members. Between them, the northern and southern wings of Methodism garnered 12 percent of their membership from the revival.

The second largest denominational group, the Baptists, gained over 92,000 members in 1858—10 percent of their total membership. The Presbyterians, the Congregationalists, and the Episcopalians also jumped.

How did this revival of 1857–58 compare with preceding revivals? It may not have had the spiritual depth of the Great Awakening of 1735 with its theological overtones. It may not have had the pervading and long-lasting influence on the life of the nation that the Revival of 1800 had. But certainly it was the most intense and fastest-spreading of the great revivals.

Three things stand out about this spiritual awakening.

- It was a laymen's movement—almost entirely. Except for Charles Finney and a few others, ministers were on the sidelines. It began an era of lay participation in the general work of the church, the Sunday school, and the YMCA.

- It was not restricted to one church denomination. At the first Fulton Street meetings, of the six persons present one was a Baptist, one a Congregationalist, one a member of the Dutch Reformed Church, and one a Presbyterian. It was the same thing wherever the revival struck. Denominational differences were forgotten in a concern for people's souls.

- As pointed out before, it was a revival of prayer. Never, since that time, have Americans bowed before the Lord so unitedly.

Revival's Lesson

What lesson does this revival teach this generation? Certainly it demonstrates how God can use one dedicated life to work out His purposes.

Jeremiah Lanphier is an inspiration to all unsung, seemingly unappreciated church workers everywhere. Surprisingly little has been written about him. He was still connected with the Old Dutch Church twenty-five years after the meeting was founded. At that time (1882), someone wrote this of him: "Out of that solitary conse-cration to the service of Christ, who can tell what results have come? . . . [He] has been most richly blessed in per-sonal work with persons who have attended the service. He quickly recognizes a stranger and seems instinctively to know the man whose heart is sore. Many a visitor has wondered when he has been greeted and addressed in words that only a tried soul could fully appreciate, 'How do you know that I am in trouble?' . . . Men under the deepest conviction have come here, and the missionary [Lanphier] has taken them to his study, there to pray with them, and to point them to the Lamb of God."

Lanphier's dedication to the work came only after a struggle and total surrender to God. He testified: "The subject was laid upon my heart and was a mat-ter of constant consideration for some time. At last I resolved to give myself to the work, and I shall never forget with what force, at the time, those words came home to my soul:

> 'Tis done, the great transaction's done,
> I am my Lord's, and He is mine;
> He drew me, and I followed on,
> Charmed to confess the voice divine."

The Revival of 1857–58 was a great national revival, but it by no means closes the story of revival in America. Revivals blazed before and after this awakening. The story of these revivals—in many respects just as significant in the history of our nation as the nationwide revivals—must be told through the lives of the faithful people of God who labored throughout the nineteenth century and into the twentieth.

four

Great Evangelists of a Golden Era

The tall, massive man with the hypnotic eyes bent low over his pulpit. "You who are now willing," he said, "to pledge to me and to Christ that you will immediately make your peace with God, please rise up. . . . You that mean that I should understand that you are committed to remain in your present attitude, not to accept Christ—those of you that are of this mind may sit still."

The people looked at one another in stunned amazement. Here was a man demanding an immediate decision. They had been brought up to believe that if you were one of the *elect*, the Holy Spirit would convert you. If you weren't, there was nothing you could do to help yourself.

The preacher had more to say. "Then you are committed. You have taken your stand. You have rejected Christ and His Gospel. . . . You may remember as long as you live that you have thus publicly committed yourselves against the Savior and said, 'We will not have this Man Christ Jesus to reign over us.'"

This was too much. Faces reddened. Women's bonnets bobbed in indignation as they turned to their neighbors with a "Well, I never—" With one accord they started for the door.

The preacher spent the next day in fasting and prayer. Rumors reached him that he was going to be tarred and feathered. But when the meeting time arrived, businesses shut down, stores closed, and everyone headed for the meetinghouse.

Young Charles G. Finney's unusual method of preaching had worked. It was the beginning of a revival at Evans Mills, New York, in 1824. And it was the beginning of an era when "the absorption in the welfare of the soul" rose to an unprecedented pitch in American history.

The nineteenth century was the golden age for evangelical Christianity in America. It began with the far-reaching Revival of 1800. Though there was a waning of religious fervor in the early 1820s, by the 1830s revivals had become part and parcel of American life.

A period of spiritual drought in the 1840s was ended by the remarkable Revival of 1857–58. After the Civil War, the revival spirit again came to the front.

During the nineteenth century, evangelists carried revival brands from generation to generation—men such as Peter Cartwright, Asahel Nettleton, Lyman Beecher, James Caughey, and Jacob Knapp. But overshadowing all others were two men: Charles G. Finney and Dwight L. Moody.

"Heathen" Studies Law

Charles G. Finney spent his boyhood in the frontier country of New York. He was, as he admitted later, "almost as destitute of religion as a heathen." Yet, when he went to study law in Adams, New York, he linked up with a Presbyterian church and listened attentively to the sermons of the Reverend George Gale. He even directed the choir. But he was not a Christian.

It was in 1821 that Finney was dramatically converted. He got interested in the Bible through references to the Old Testament laws in his legal books. He bought a Bible and through reading it became intellectually convinced of the truth of Christianity. But the question remained—should he become a Christian?

One autumn morning he was on his way to his office when he was stopped in his tracks by an inward voice that seemed to say, "Will you accept it now, today?" Instead of going to his office, Finney went off into the woods. Reaching a spot where he thought no one would see him, he knelt down.

He tried to pray but could not. He was just about to give up when he heard a rustling and looked up in alarm to see if someone had discovered him. Suddenly, he realized how great was his pride. Remembering the words of Jeremiah 29:13, "And you will seek Me and find Me, when you search for Me with all your heart," he cried out, "Lord, I take you at your word."

Finney left the woods in a lighthearted mood. He didn't quite understand what had happened to him.

That evening in the back of his law office he was overcome with a sense of unutterable ecstasy. He later wrote, "The Holy Spirit descended upon me in a manner that seemed to go through me, body and soul. I could feel the impression, like a wave of electricity, going through and through me. Indeed it seemed to come in waves and waves of liquid love; for I could not express it in any other way. It seemed like the very breath of God. I can recollect distinctly that it seemed to fan me, like immense wings."

Finney dropped his law studies the next day and went about the town telling what the Lord had done for him. A revival began immediately.

After studying theology with his pastor, Finney was commissioned by a women's missionary society to preach in western New York. Beginning with Evans Mills, town after town experienced revival.

While preaching at Evans Mills, Finney took time out to be married. After "a day or two," he left his wife in Whitestown to go back to Evans Mills, intending to return in a week with a rig to carry their household effects. As it turned out, he was gone six months, for he found little revivals popping up all around Evans Mills. He felt he could not take the time that winter to get his wife.

Early in the spring, however, he set out in horse and sleigh for Whitestown. On the way, when he had to stop to have his horse shod, the people of that town begged him to preach. He did so, and a revival started. Someone else had to be sent to fetch Finney's wife.

Wherever he went, people turned out en masse. He preached out of doors, in barns, and in schoolhouses. Men left their plows in the fields to come to the meetinghouse in work clothes. Invariably, Finney's sermons were followed immediately by confession, repentance, tears, and many conversions.

"Promoting" Revivals

Finney didn't believe in sitting passively waiting for God to send a revival. He set out to promote revivals; he believed God wanted him to do this.

In one town he found the meetinghouse locked up. He persuaded a woman to let him use her parlor for a meeting at which he preached to thirteen people. Next, he got permission to use the schoolhouse on Sunday. In the meantime he walked around the village and was horrified at the cursing and swearing. The atmosphere, he said, "seemed to me to be poison." On Sunday, however, the schoolhouse was full. Finney rebuked the towns-people for their profanity. He told them they seemed "to howl blasphemy about the streets like hellhounds." At first angered, the people soon began to confess their sins. The man who had locked the meetinghouse gave in and gave Finney the key. A revival was underway.

A spirit of prayer marked every Finney revival. Converts prayed all night for others. When Finney was in town, it was common for Christians to fall on their knees in prayer whenever they met. Finney assured people that God would answer prayer if they fulfilled the conditions upon which He promised to answer prayer.

Finney himself depended utterly on prayer. He said, "Unless I had the spirit of prayer, I could do nothing. If even for a day or an hour I lost the spirit of grace and supplication, I found myself unable to preach with power and efficiency or to win souls by personal conversation."

During the winter of 1828–1829, Finney was in Philadelphia. A number of lumbermen who had come down the Delaware River on rafts of lumber were converted. They went back into the wilderness, where there were no schools, no churches, no ministers, and touched off a backwoods revival in which 5,000 people were converted.

The next year, Finney conducted a revival in Rochester, New York, during which 1,000 persons were converted. Within another year or so, 1,500 towns and cities were affected.

In 1832, Finney was called to a pastorate in New York City and while there organized the Broadway Tabernacle. It was only ten years since Finney had been touched by God and had gone out to turn towns upside down. He ought to have been well satisfied, but Finney was troubled. His health was beginning to decline. It seemed that the revivals were falling off. *Perhaps my work is coming to an end*, Finney thought. He decided to take a voyage to the Mediterranean.

On the way home Finney was beside himself. He prayed night and day and paced restlessly on deck. At length, "After a day of unspeakable wrestling and agony in my soul, just at night, the subject cleared up to my mind. The Spirit led me to believe that all would come out right and that God had yet a work for me to do; that I might be at rest; that the Lord would go forward with His work and give me strength to take any part in it that He desired."

God did indeed have much more for Finney to do. Back in New York, he gave a series of lectures on revivals. These were later published as *Finney's Lectures on Revival*. Twelve thousand copies were sold as fast as they could be printed. The book was translated into several languages. A London publisher sold 80,000 volumes, and the lectures were instrumental in promoting revivals in England, Scotland, Wales, and Canada.

Soon after this, Finney accepted the professorship of theology at Oberlin College in Ohio, later becoming president. He continued with evangelistic work and made two visits to London, where as many as 1,500 persons at a time attended his meetings. He served at Oberlin to within a few weeks of his death in 1875.

An Immediate Verdict

What was the strength of Finney's preaching? Other evangelists believed ministers should not try to "get up" a revival. Preach the Gospel, they said, and depend on the Holy Spirit to bring about an awakening. Finney appealed for an immediate decision for Jesus Christ. He directed his sermon to each hearer personally. He had no patience with preachers who preached "about other people and sins of other people, instead of addressing them and saying, 'You are guilty of these sins,' and 'The Lord requires this of you.'"

Finney did not agree with the "Old School" Presbyterian view that man was unable to do anything about his salvation but could only wait for the Holy Spirit to give him a new heart. No, said Finney. Salvation is for everyone, for the "whosoever will." A man has free will to accept or to reject Christ. True, it was the work of the Holy Spirit to convict sinners (often through a preacher), but in the end, the sinner had to take the step of faith.

Finney was severely criticized for certain "new measures" he put into use in his revivals. He prayed for sinners by name. He introduced the "anxious seat," a bench in the front of the church to which people who were in the struggle of rebirth were invited. He permitted women to pray in public. He spoke in everyday language. He used assistants to speak to people about their soul's welfare. All these things were highly unconventional.

While a pastor in New York, Finney became convinced through studying the Bible that "an altogether higher and more stable form of Christian life was attainable and was the privilege of all Christians." He preached his doctrine of "entire sanctification" at Oberlin College, although he did not profess to have found the experience he taught for some years. To Finney, "perfection" meant perfect trust and consecration that could enable a Christian to live without "known sin." It did not mean freedom from troublesome physical and mental appetites or from error and prejudice.

Unfortunately, Finney lived to see this doctrine carried to extremes. By 1857, he was denouncing those who "having begun in the Spirit . . . try to become perfect in the flesh."

Charles G. Finney might be called the father of modern evangelism. Many owe a debt to him for his pioneering in the task of promoting revivals. One of these was a man whose labors began when Finney's work was coming to a close—the great evangelist of the cities, Dwight L. Moody.

God Kindles a Fire

In 1856, a stocky young man from Northfield, Massachusetts, arrived in Chicago seeking to make a fortune of $100,000. Soon he was well on his way to his goal as a successful shoe salesman. But something happened to change the direction of his life.

After working hard all week as a traveling salesman, Moody, who had been converted at the age of seventeen by his Sunday school teacher, was superintending a Sunday school he had built up from a class of boys. One day a fellow teacher, who was deathly ill, came to him. He told Moody he was going home to die, but he was troubled because he had never led any of the girls in his class to Christ. Moody consented to go with the teacher to visit each girl. For the first time Moody prayed for the salvation of a person, and his prayers were answered. One by one the girls were converted. Moody called the girls of the class together for a prayer meeting on the night before the teacher was to leave. The touching prayers of the girls greatly affected Moody.

Moody said later, "God kindled a fire in my soul that has never gone out. The height of my ambition had been to be a successful merchant, and if I had known that meeting was going to take that ambition out of me, I might not have gone."

Shortly thereafter Moody gave up his job to devote himself fully to the Lord's work. When a speaker failed to show up at a Sunday school convention, he gave his first public sermon, and over sixty were converted. He was active in YMCA work. During the Civil War, he did chaplain work at Camp Douglas, just south of Chicago. He carried on his regular Sunday school work, and he started Sunday evening services.

In 1867, he went to England to hear the great preacher Charles Spurgeon. There he met young Henry Moorhouse, "The Boy Preacher," who returned to America with him and gave a series of sermons at Moody's church on God's love. For six straight nights the young man preached on the same verse: John 3:16. He went through the Bible from Genesis to Revelation to prove that in all ages God loved the world.

Moody's reaction: "I never knew up to that time that God loved us so much. This heart of mine began to thaw out. I could not keep back the tears. It was like news from a far country. I just drank it in."

Moody's preaching changed. "I used to preach that God was behind the sinner with a double-edged sword ready to hew him down. I have got done with that. I preach now that God is behind him with love, and he is running away from the God of love." After that, Moody was to be an expositor of Scripture. He realized how inadequate he was in education and experience for the task of preaching. Yet by 1865, he was pastor of his own church on Illinois Street.

Moody Seeks Power

Two women used to sit in Moody's meetings in the front row. He could see by the expressions on their faces that they were praying. At the close of the services they would say to him, "We have been praying for you."

"Why don't you pray for the people?" Moody would ask.

"Because you need the power of the Spirit," they said.

Moody said years later, "I need the power? Why, I thought I had power. I had the largest congregations in Chicago, and there were many conversions. I was in a sense satisfied."

The women kept right on praying, and Moody was filled with a great heart hunger. While Moody was in this restless condition, the Great Chicago Fire laid the city in ashes in October 1871, destroying his church and his home. Afterward he went to New York to raise money for a new church. While there he had the crowning spiritual experience of his life.

Moody only said this about it: "My heart was not in the work of begging. I could not appeal. I was crying all the time that God would fill me with His Spirit. Well, one day in the city of New York—oh, what a day!—I cannot describe it, I seldom refer to it; it is almost too sacred an experience to name. Paul had an experience of which he never spoke for fourteen years. I can only say that God revealed himself to me, and I had such an experience of His love that I had to ask Him to stay His hand. I went to preaching again. The sermons were not different; I did not present any new truths, and yet hundreds were converted."

Moody was unprepared for the result of his spiritual renewal. He went to England in June 1872, not intending to do any evangelistic work. However, the pastor of a North London church persuaded him to preach on a Sunday. To Moody, the morning service seemed dead and cold. But at the evening service a hush came upon the people. Moody couldn't understand it. When he asked all who would like to become Christians to rise that he might pray for them, it seemed as if the whole audience stood.

Moody said to himself, "These people don't understand me. They don't know what I mean." To make sure, he asked them to go to the inquiry room. Everyone who had stood filed into the inquiry room. Again Moody asked them to rise if they really wanted to become Christians. They all got up again. Not knowing what to do, Moody told all who *really* were in earnest to meet with the pastor the next night.

Moody left London, but on Tuesday he received an urgent message to return to the church. In the Monday evening meeting, there had been more inquirers than on Sunday! Moody went back and held meetings for ten days. As a result, 400 people were taken into the church.

He found out later that the way had been prepared by a disabled woman who had been praying for revival in the church. She had read about Moody in the newspaper and asked God to send him to her church.

Moody believed that it was this revival that carried him back to England the next year with a singing partner, Ira D. Sankey. They took England and the British Isles by storm. When they returned to America, a revival started in Brooklyn. Five thousand people filled the building three times a day. In Philadelphia, 13,000 heard them in each meeting. For ten weeks they held forth in New York City while 500 ushers tried to handle long lines of people trying to get into the Hippodrome.

Like Finney, Moody was a man of prayer, and he believed prayer was necessary to revival.

At one of his Hippodrome meetings in New York, Moody said, "Now, won't a thousand of you Christians go into the Fourth Avenue Hall and pray for this meeting and let those outside have your seats?" Only a few left. "Not half enough," Moody said. "I want a great many more to go out. I see many of you here every night, and if I knew your names I'd call you out." Moody was often disturbed because Christians occupied seats he thought the unconverted should fill.

Prisoner Converted

Boston, Chicago, Cleveland, St. Louis, Denver, San Francisco—everywhere Moody went, throngs gathered to hear him and thousands were converted. In St. Louis, a notorious prisoner was converted through reading one of Moody's sermons in a newspaper.

When Moody died in 1899, he left behind lasting monuments—a girls' school in Northfield, a boys' school at Mount Hermon, and his Bible institute in Chicago. But even more important, he left a spiritual monument in an estimated 1 million souls won to the kingdom of God.

Moody also perfected efficient techniques that characterized the urban mass evangelistic campaigns that early twentieth-century evangelists such as Reuben Torrey, Wilbur Chapman, B. Fay Mills, Sam Jones, George Stuart, W. E. Biederwolf, and Billy Sunday utilized.

How would you compare Finney and Moody? Finney was better educated, perhaps intellectually superior, certainly more influential in the field of theology. Moody never considered himself to be a great preacher. He told a newspaperman, "I am the most overestimated man in this country. For some reason the people look upon me as a great man, but I am only a lay preacher and have little learning."

Still, they both spoke in the everyday language of the common man. They spoke so that the least educated could understand the Gospel. They both avoided controversies and discouraged sectarianism. They both depended upon prayer. Most important, they were both consumed with a love for Christ and a zeal to bring men and women to a knowledge of Him.

In every age, revivals have been scorned, derided, condemned. The revival spirit of the nineteenth century was blamed for causing controversies and divisions among Christians, for fostering confusion and disorder in worship, for being responsible for doctrinal heresies.

These criticisms cannot be answered by denying them, for there is an element of truth in each one. Yet they can be countered with facts that are agreed to by historians. The revival spirit of the nineteenth century made Christian liberty, Christian equality, and Christian brotherhood the passion of the land. Slavery, poverty, and greed were attacked as never before. Home and foreign mission efforts, Christian philanthropy, and moral reform became the concern of almost every converted soul.

Though it was true that the nineteenth century saw divisions in churches and the multiplication of sects, it also saw a tremendous growth in the church as a whole. At the beginning of the century, one in sixteen persons in the United States was a church member; at its close one out of every four belonged to evangelical Protestant churches.

five

Twentieth-Century Revivals

At the beginning of the twentieth century, the pendulum of sentiment toward revival in America had swung against what had been perceived as an overemphasis on the emotional and an underestimate of the rational element in spiritual experience. It is said that critics—both in the church as well as without—embalmed revivalism, buried it, and sat on its gravestone. Emotion was all but squeezed out of religion in the denominations that once strongly promoted revivals.

But emotion had not been squeezed out of mankind. Men and women found outlets in this new century of jazz bands, movies, and radio. The pursuit of material success and the pleasures of the senses, the idolizing of popular entertainers, and the proliferation of organized crime became everyday themes. One might have thought that the devastation and horrors of World War I would lead to a national moral reformation, but rather it led to the Roaring Twenties and widespread moral decline. The nation's total wealth more than doubled between 1920 and 1929, yet when that economic boom crashed in 1929 and was followed by the Great Depression, there were few calls for a national revival.

A major focus within the Church was the ongoing struggle between conservative evangelical theology and the rampant liberalism that infiltrated mainline denominations. Nevertheless, the twentieth century witnessed several significant revivals comparable to revivals of the eighteenth and nineteenth centuries, with each one playing an important role in keeping the streams of revival flowing.

Revivals of 1905–1906

Reports of the powerful Welsh Revival of 1904, during which 100,000 people were converted in one year within Wales, spread to Welsh immigrants who had settled in Pennsylvania, and in December 1904 a revival broke out in Wilkes-Barre. Edwin Orr wrote that local revivals burned throughout New England, stating that "the movement was characterized by an intense sensation of the presence of God in the congregations, as in the Welsh Revival. . . . The churches were obviously in the midst of a revival of greater power and extent than

New England had known since 1858." In Philadelphia, the Methodists reported 10,000 converts by early 1905.

Reports of the revival were far-reaching—Colorado, Michigan, Nebraska, North and South Carolina. It was "the most remarkable revival ever known in the city. . . . Fifty-eight of the leading business firms of the city are closed [for prayer] at the noon hour," according to Louisville papers. Almost a thousand businessmen, said the press in Atlanta, joined in prayer for the Holy Spirit to revive their churches. In March 2, 1905, the *Christian Advocate* newspaper stated that 600 people gave their lives to Christ during a January revival in Redwood Falls, Minnesota (population of 2,000), despite temperatures of twenty-two below!

Billy Sunday

In the early 1900s, Billy Sunday, a popular professional baseball player turned preacher, had become the nation's most famous evangelist. Though his countless crusades drew crowds in the thousands across the nation, his preaching style was often heavily criticized as being overly dramatic and unconventional, and his vocabulary uncultured. In answer, Sunday said, "I want to preach the gospel so plainly that men can come from the factories and not have to bring a dictionary." At the close of his messages he would invite those who wanted to put their faith in Christ to "walk the sawdust trail" to the front of the wooden tabernacles that were often constructed specifically for his meetings. With the administrative help of his wife, Sunday's evangelistic staff was organized with advance men, those who make arrangements in advance of their employer's appearances; a song leader; a choir; secretaries; and local volunteers, and his staff raised expenses in advance of his meetings.

On November 12, 1916, 70,000 people came to hear Sunday preach in Boston, with 15,000 being turned away for lack of space within the temporary tabernacle that had been constructed. During the ten-week Boston crusade, he drew an estimated 1.3 million people and nearly 65,000 made a profession of faith. His Boston sermons that spoke against the vices of alcohol are said to have helped win congressional passage of the Eighteenth Amendment to the Constitution that prohibited "the manufacture, sale, or transportation of intoxicating liquors."

The height of Sunday's career was in 1917 during a ten-week revival in New York City where he preached to over 1 million people in a wooden 18,000-seat tabernacle. An estimated 98,000 people declared their faith in Christ.

It is estimated that Sunday preached nearly 20,000 sermons from 1896 to 1935, sometimes preaching more than twenty times a week during his prime. Even as his career waned, over 475,000 people in Columbia, South Carolina, attended his six weeks of meetings in 1923. Sunday is said to have preached to 100 million people, mostly without the use of audio equipment, with an estimated 1 million of those "hitting the sawdust trail." No American evangelist had ever preached to so many millions.

The Azusa Street Revival

In 1906, the modern Pentecostal Movement was born in Los Angeles. In February, William J. Seymour, an African-American pastor and son of former slaves, had come to Los Angeles as a pastoral candidate. He was rejected for preaching that speaking in tongues was the first biblical evidence of the baptism of the Holy Spirit, even though he had not experienced it himself. So he began prayer meetings in a cottage home and teaching a small group that "the second blessing" of God was about to come to all of them. It is said that Seymour sometimes prayed for hours a day for the power of the Spirit to come.

On April 9, 1906, it was reported that "the power fell," and over the following days Seymour and several other people began to praise God in "unknown tongues." It was seen by many as a present-day fulfillment of the day of Pentecost in Acts 2. News of the speaking in tongues spread quickly, and a racially diverse crowd grew so quickly that a new meeting place was found in an abandoned downtown church at 312 Azusa Street, which a newspaper referred to as a "tumbledown shack." Three services a day, seven days a week, continued here with blacks, whites, Latinos, and Asians seeking salvation and "the baptism of the Holy Ghost." Not only was such diversity unusual at the time, but the more the newspapers ridiculed these uncommon meetings, the more people from all backgrounds—believers and unbelievers, professors and those with less education, rich and poor—were drawn together. Within a few months, anywhere from 300 to 1,500 would attempt to fit into the forty-by-sixty-foot wood-frame building.

People from across America and around the world heard the curious news of the Azusa Street Revival, and thousands came to witness it for themselves. They found lengthy, mostly unscripted, spontaneous services—even the preaching was often not prepared in advance and the singing mostly a cappella. There were many spoken testimonies, altar calls for salvation or the baptism of the Holy Spirit, laying on of hands and prayer for the sick, and firsthand reports of healing. Some people shouted throughout the meetings, and others were "slain in the Spirit" or "fell under the power," but there were also times of silence as well as singing in tongues.

The revival continued for about three years. While the number of regular attenders remained relatively small—in the hundreds—it was the thousands of people who visited the church and were touched by their experiences who gave this revival its significance. Thousands left Azusa Street intent upon evangelizing in their home churches and locales, armed with teachings of salvation as a personal experience, the baptism of the Spirit, holiness, healing, and a strong emphasis on the imminent second coming of Christ. It was reported that thirty-eight missionaries were sent out from

Azusa in October 1906 and that within two years the movement had spread to over fifty nations, including Mexico, Hong Kong, China, Ceylon, India, Britain, Germany, Holland, Egypt, Liberia, Syria, Palestine, and South Africa.

No one could have imagined that the Azusa Street Revival would be the catalyst of the Pentecostal Movement and the later Charismatic Movement. Pentecostalism has been called "the third force in Christendom," being a movement that was neither Roman Catholic nor mainline Protestant in origin. What happened at Azusa Street helped to chip away at some of the racial barriers within the Church as well as bring together people from all levels of society into a more unified body and elevate women's ministries. The ensuing Pentecostal Movement brought into focus the gifts of the Holy Spirit and the empowerment of the Church to follow in the steps of the Christians of Acts.

Several major Pentecostal denominations, including the Assemblies of God in Springfield, Missouri, trace their historic roots to the impact of the Azusa Street Revival on their founders. The effects of this revival spread to almost every country in the world. There are an estimated 580 million Pentecostal and charismatic believers across the globe, and it is the fastest-growing branch of Christianity today.

Post–World War II Revivals

After World War II, a new generation of strong evangelical Christian leaders emerged, bringing a wide expansion of evangelical activity and organizations. In 1943, the *Old Fashioned Revival Hour* was the single most popular national radio program, with 20 million weekly listeners. Parachurch organizations were formed, such as Young Life by Jim Rayburn in 1941, which later became the base for Billy Graham's revivals. The National Association of Evangelicals was founded in 1942. Bill Bright began Campus Crusade for Christ in 1951. The founding of Fuller Seminary in 1947 and *Christianity Today* magazine in 1956 represented the growing evangelical influence in society. The founding of World Relief (1944), World Vision (1950), and Compassion International (1952) represented the humanitarian side.

Henrietta Mears was one of the most influential Christian leaders of the twentieth century and the director of Christian education at the First Presbyterian

Church of Hollywood, California. Starting around 1946, the Forest Home Retreat Center, which she founded, saw significant spiritual awakenings during conferences held there. Thousands of college students returned to their campuses having made a complete surrender to Christ and the indwelling power of the Holy Spirit and taking with them a passion to win their fellow students for Christ. Billy Graham received a fresh touch of the spirit of revival here, as did Bill Bright and Jim Rayburn, along with many other leaders who stepped into ministry and mission areas.

College revivals started as early as 1946. After Edwin Orr taught a course on spiritual awakenings at Wheaton College in 1949, a day of prayer in February 1950 was set aside to ask God to "open the windows of heaven and pour out a blessing," and that is exactly what happened. For the following several days, there was an extraordinary sense of God's presence that brought a deep conviction of sin and repentance. What started as a testimonial meeting went on for forty-eight straight hours, with well over 1,300 students and faculty members joining in. Nearly all the students stepped up to the pulpit at least once and confessed their sins and their commitment to Christ. This revival made the national news as well as being reported on in *Time* magazine, sparking other college revivals throughout America.

There were noteworthy college awakenings at Bethel College, Northern Baptist Theological Seminary, and North Park College. Both Lee College and Asbury College experienced similar revivals to Wheaton College in February 1950, with many days of confession of sin and tears as well as rejoicing as hundreds gave their lives to Christ. At Lee College in Cleveland, Tennessee, which is the Church of God's oldest educational institution, gifts of the Spirit were poured out upon students and faculty members.

Billy Graham

In 1949, Billy Graham had been rising in prominence among American evangelicals. However, his renowned evangelistic career burst onto the scene during his Los Angeles Crusade in late September 1949. Originally, the nightly meetings had been scheduled for three weeks but were extended to eight weeks, and during that time more than 350,000 people crammed into the enormous tent to hear Graham. Millions of people across the nation read about the crusade's success in newspapers. He gained further exposure and stature through nationally publicized crusades in Boston, Washington, and other major cities and through his *Hour of Decision* radio program, which began in 1950. Also in 1950, Graham officially incorporated the Billy Graham Evangelistic Association. For the next four decades, he traveled fulltime as an evangelist, holding revival meetings in every major city in the United States.

His 1954 meetings in London propelled him onto the international stage. From March 1 through the closing meeting on May 22, crowds flooded the crusade. On the closing night, Wembley Stadium was filled to overflowing with 120,000 people. So many other people wanted to be there that an extra afternoon meeting was arranged at White City Stadium, drawing in another 65,000 people. More than 2 million people attended the meetings, and nearly 40,000 made a commitment to Christ.

During the summer of 1957, Graham's sixteen weeks of nightly revival meetings in New York City attracted more than 2 million people to Madison Square Garden. On several nights, the ABC television network broadcast the meetings live on prime time, with millions nationwide tuning in to watch. By the end of the campaign, 55,000 people had made professions of faith.

On the last day of Graham's 1963 three-week revival at the Los Angeles Memorial Coliseum, over 134,000 people crowded in to hear him, the largest crowd ever assembled in that coliseum. An estimated 215 million people attended his nearly 400 crusades in 185 countries, and countless millions more viewed them on television. Nearly 3 million responded to the invitation to receive Christ that he offered at the end of his sermons.

The Charismatic Movement

During the late 1960s and early 1970s, more revivals developed. One was the Charismatic Movement that spread far beyond Pentecostal churches to college campuses, the Catholic Church, and mainline denominations. The beginning of the movement is usually dated to April 3, 1960, when Dennis Bennett, an Episcopal priest in California, described his experience of the Holy Spirit to his parish. It marked the beginning of a widespread outpouring of the Spirit at a grassroots level that cannot be sourced to one leader or group.

Before this time, it was typically expected that if you were a member of a mainstream church and began to express Pentecostal views, you would either leave your church on your own or you'd be asked to leave. However, in the 1960s, the emphasis on the baptism or filling of the Holy Spirit and gifts of the Spirit was gaining acceptance among mainline denominations. Thus many who were caught up in the Charismatic Movement chose to remain in their original churches.

The movement takes its name from the Greek word *charismata*, meaning "a gift of grace." Most often this word is used for the gifts of the Holy Spirit that enable the believer to fulfill his or her calling. Central to the Charismatic Movement is the teaching that all the spiritual gifts in the New Testament (see 1 Corinthians 12:4–11) are given to believers to be experienced and practiced today. This belief challenges many denominations' traditional teaching that certain gifts, such as gifts of prophecy, healing, working of miracles, and speaking in tongues, died out with the apostolic period of the early church.

While many charismatics remained within their mainline churches, one of the most visible results of the movement is the charismatic Vineyard Christian

Fellowships. In 1977, John Wimber began pastoring a small fellowship of believers and preaching about spiritual gifts and praying for hundreds of people to be healed before the first healing came. When the healings began to happen, they became a regular part of the Vineyard ministry. In 1980, the congregation experienced a revival when a young preacher asked those under the age of twenty-five to come forward. He then prayed for the Holy Spirit to come, and hundreds of young people fell to the floor, weeping and speaking in tongues. In the next four months, hundreds of new converts were baptized. Ministering in the Spirit's power became a regular part of their international teaching ministry. Today there are over 2,400 Vineyard-associated churches around the world in 95 countries. Over 300 million people in the world are considered charismatic Christians.

Jesus Movement

During the late 1960s, the Jesus Movement began in the counterculture centers of California, and throughout the 1970s it spread primarily through young people across America and other parts of the Western world.

In San Francisco's Haight-Ashbury district, a couple opened a Christian coffeehouse called the Living Room, where disillusioned young people began finding Christ. Soon other similar Christian coffeehouses sprang up and engaged in evangelistic outreach. Mass baptisms of hundreds of young people were held in the Pacific Ocean with outdoor meetings and teams witnessing on the beaches. The simple message of the "Jesus People" was to turn from the drugs, immorality, and radical politics of the day and find Jesus Christ as one's personal Savior and Lord and believe the Bible as God's Word.

By 1971, the movement had found its way into city streets from coast to coast, with thousands of young people gathered in rooms, large meeting places, and theaters to preach, sing, witness, and repent. "Street Christians," young lives changed by the love and power of God, began to spontaneously witness to their dedication to "follow Jesus." New ministries and church groups such as Calvary Chapel emerged that did not fit traditional denominations. In June 1971, *Time* magazine carried a cover article on the Jesus Movement as the religious story of the year. A one-day Jesus festival in Dallas in the summer of 1972 drew 150,000 people.

Not surprisingly, this revival spread to hundreds of college campuses and lead to, most notably, the 1970 Asbury College Revival. On February 3, the regular morning chapel saw God move in the students in such a way that many came weeping to the front to kneel in repentance and confession of sin while others gave testimonies and sang songs. Classes were canceled as the auditorium filled with over 1,000 people. By midnight, over 500 still remained praying and worshiping. Hundreds committed their lives to Christ that day. Lectures were canceled the next day as the chapel filled again with more of the same.

News of the revival spread instantly, and within a week invitations from other colleges and churches were coming from around the country. In the first week after the revival began, outreach teams of students visited sixteen states by invitation and saw thousands of conversions. Almost half the 1,000-member student body at Asbury was involved in witnessing teams. By the end of May 1970, some 2,000 witness teams of students had gone out from the college and adjacent theological seminary. There were 130 colleges, seminaries, and Bible schools impacted by the students' "revival outreach" trips.

Wherever teams went, the revival spread. The college remained the center of the revival with meetings continuing at night and on weekends, along with spontaneous prayer groups meeting. Hundreds of people visited the college to see and participate in this revival. They took reports and their own testimonies of changed lives back to their churches or colleges.

The Jesus Movement was different than revivals of the past in that it primarily occurred among young people and extended throughout America and parts of the Western world. Similar to the Charismatic Movement, it also differed from previous historic revivals that typically focused on a few prominent leaders. Certainly there were many pastors and musicians who gained prominence during the Jesus Movement, but none were the key to the movement. It was truly as Jesus said: "The wind blows where it wishes, and you hear the sound of it, but cannot tell where it comes from and where it goes" (John 3:8).

By the end of 1975, the Jesus Movement was in decline, but it propelled a whole new generation of young people into ministries and missions. Dynamic new evangelical leaders have made a long-term impact on the Church as well as new styles of worship with praise choruses and worship bands and new music, creating the contemporary Christian music industry.

The number of conversions resulting from the Jesus Movement has been estimated at 3 million.

Revivals throughout the 1990s

Starting at Howard Payne University in February 1995 under the preaching of Henry Blackaby, a Southern Baptist, revival came to the campus with hundreds of students coming under strong conviction that they were not living holy lives. Subsequent revivals soon swept across other campuses and churches across America. Also in the mid-1990s, a series of controversial revivals impacted the lives of hundreds of thousands of people—the Toronto Blessing, the Melbourne Revival, and the Modesto Revival. Also among those was the Pensacola Outpouring, which reported 100,000 conversions in two years.

Previous to these revivals, the Promise Keepers began a national revival in 1991 when 4,200 men assembled at the University of Colorado to be encouraged to live up to their calling as godly men, husbands, and fathers. In 1992, over 22,000 men came together, and in 1993, the number increased to 50,000 men. In the following years, the conference schedule was expanded to include other city stadium events throughout the United States and millions more men attended. The conference particularly touched Christian men's culture. In October 1997, between 600,000 and 800,000 men gathered on the National Mall in Washington, DC, marking the revival's high point. By the close of 2000, Promise Keepers reported 5 million had attended 100 conferences, and the movement had spread from the stadiums into the Church.

A Final Word

Today, many are once again seeing that religion must be personal and individual or it is not true religion at all. The words Jonathan Edwards wrote in defense of the Great Awakening are just as true today: "True religion is a powerful thing . . . a ferment, a vigorous engagedness of the heart." Revivals have accomplished what God placed His Church into the world to accomplish, bringing countless men and women into a personal relationship with Jesus Christ. Revival has been, and still is, the result of the moving of the Holy Spirit, repentance, prayer, and dedication. We are reminded that nationwide spiritual movements have begun when God's children have fallen to their knees and sought power from on high. The God of Edwards, Lanphier, Finney, Moody, and Graham is our God today!